D1216997

COUNTRIES IN OUR WORLD

SOUTH KOREA
IN OUR WORLD

Jim Pipe

A⁺
Smart Apple Media

Published by Smart Apple Media
P.O. Box 3263, Mankato, Minnesota 56002

Printed in the United States of America at Corporate Graphics, in North Mankato, Minnesota.

Published by arrangement with the Watts Publishing Group LTD, London.

Library of Congress Cataloging-in-Publication Data
Pipe, Jim, 1966-
  South Korea in our world / by Jim Pipe.
     p. cm. -- (Countries in our world)
  Includes index.
  Summary: "Describes the geography, landscape, economy, government, and culture of South Korea today and discusses South Korea's influence of and relations with the rest of the world"--Provided by publisher.
  ISBN 978-1-59920-433-8 (library binding)
  1. Korea (South)--Juvenile literature. I. Title.
  DS902.P57 2012
  951.95--dc22
                                        2010035507

1305
3-2011

9 8 7 6 5 4 3 2 1

Produced for Franklin Watts by
White-Thomson Publishing Ltd
Series consultant: Rob Bowden
Editor: Sonya Newland
Designer: Amy Sparks
Picture researcher: Sonya Newland

Picture Credits
Corbis: 9 (Atlantide Phototravel), 13 (Paul A. Souders), 17 (Yonhap News Agency/epa), 19 (Kim Kyung-Hoon/Reuters), 20 (Jeon Heon-Kyun/epa), 21 (Nayan Sthakiya), 26 (Lee Jin-man/Pool/Reuters), 28 (epa), 29 (Yonhap); **Dreamstime:** 6 (Jarn Godfrey), 7 (Hendrik Halianto), 12 (Ragsac19), 18 (Richard Lindie); **EASI-Images/Rob Bowden:** 5, 8, 14, 15, 10; **iStock:** 11 (Min-Gyu Seong); **Photoshot:** 10 (Xinhua); **Photolibrary:** 22 (Photononstop); **Shutterstock:** Cover (Mastering Microstock), 16 (Gina Smith), 23 (Andrey Shchekalev); **UN Photo:** 27 (Paulo Filgueiras); **US Army:** 25 (Edward N. Johnson).

Contents

South Korea is a small country in northeast Asia best known for its economic success. It has transformed itself into a wealthy and developed country in less than 50 years. Most Koreans live in large cities packed with giant factories and towering office and apartment blocks, yet South Korea is also famous for its natural beauty.

One Peninsula, Two Countries

South Korea covers the southern end of the Korean Peninsula, which juts into the sea northwest of Japan. To the east is the Sea of Japan and to the west is the Yellow Sea. To the north lies North Korea, a separate country. People in both nations share the same language and culture, but North Korea is a communist country while South Korea is a democracy. An old proverb describes Korea as "a shrimp between whales," because it is surrounded by much larger neighbors—China, Russia, and Japan.

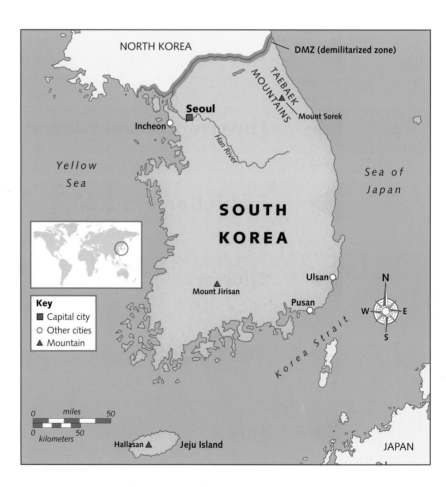

▲ *South Korea only has a land border with North Korea. Its nearest neighbor to the south is Japan, which lies across the Korea Strait.*

BASIC DATA

Official name: Republic of Korea

Capital: Seoul

Size: 38,023 sq miles (98,480 sq km)

Population: 48,636,068 (2010 est.)

Currency: Won

An "Asian Tiger"

Since the 1960s, the economy in South Korea has grown rapidly, earning the nickname "Asian Tiger." It is now the fourth-largest economy in Asia and the fifteenth-largest in the world. This growth slowed following the worldwide economic crisis that began in 2008, yet South Korea is still home to some of the world's biggest companies, including well-known brand names such as Samsung and Hyundai. The country is also among the world's top exporters. Korean electronics, cars, ships, steel, shoes, and chemicals are sold all over the globe.

▶ *South Korean cities are full of energy. The bustling Itaewon district in Seoul is famous for its shopping and nightlife.*

North and South

Politics in South Korea are still greatly influenced by the past. After World War II (1939–45), the country was divided between Russian and U.S. forces. In 1950, war broke out between North and South Korea. More than 50 years later, there is still a demilitarized zone (DMZ), a 2.5-mile (4 km) wide strip of land between the two countries, with border guards always on the alert. Tensions remain high due to North Korea's nuclear weapons testing. In 2010, tensions grew even higher when artillery fire was exchanged between North and South.

▼ *South Korea's cities are packed with people. During the summer, thousands descend on the beaches at Pusan, the country's second-largest city.*

A Fast Pace of Life

In the last 30 years, there have been enormous changes in South Korea. As the economy grew, more people moved to the cities. Today, millions of South Koreans are packed into a few cities where ancient buildings sit next to modern skyscrapers. Hard-working and highly skilled, the South Koreans live life in the fast lane. On city streets people cry: *Bali, bali!* ("Hurry! Hurry!") Cars and trucks jam the roads, contributing to South Korea having one of the worst air pollution problems in the world.

THE HOME OF...

Barbecues

The Korean word for barbecue, *pulgogi*, means "fire meat." This refers to the way beef, pork, and chicken are cooked on a grill rather than how spicy the dish is. First, the raw meat is soaked in a salty sauce. Then, it is cooked at the table on charcoal or gas grills, often by the diners themselves. Lettuce is wrapped around the meat to make a tasty sandwich.

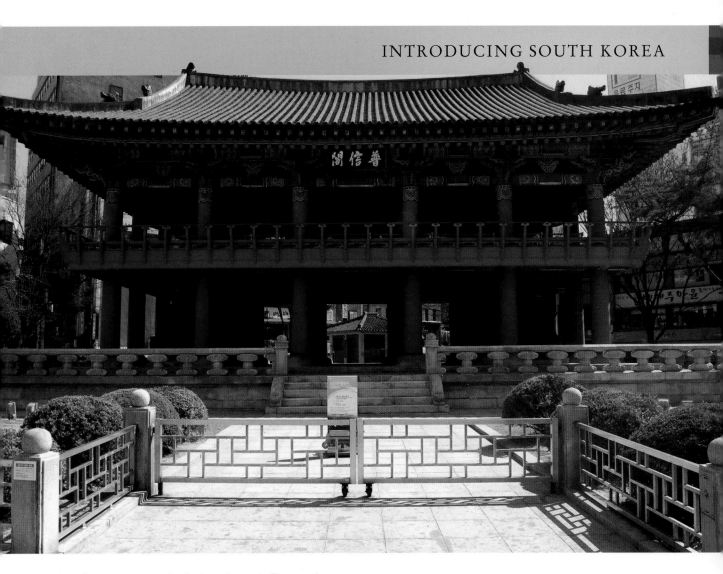

▲ *South Korean temple designs have influenced those in other Buddhist countries, particulary Japan.*

Korea and the World

Although South Korea is buzzing with city life, there is a lot more to the country than factories and industry. Traditional Korean culture and its Buddhist heritage have had a big influence on other Asian countries over the centuries. Influences include temple architecture, pottery, and painting. Today, South Korean pop music, TV shows, and films are very popular all over Asia. South Korean communities around the world have also helped the spread of Korean customs and culture.

IT STARTED HERE

Moveable Type

Inventor Choe Yun-ui invented moveable type in 1234—more than 200 years before it was used in Europe. This system of printing uses metal type that can easily be rearranged to form different sentences. It allows books to be printed quickly in large numbers.

Landscapes and Environment

South Korea takes up the lower half of the Korean Peninsula, a 621-mile (1,000 km) piece of land surrounded by sea on three sides. South Korea itself is slightly larger than the state of Indiana, and about 70 percent is covered in mountains. Most people live on coastal plains and river valleys on the southern and western coasts.

Mountains

Early European visitors said that South Korea looked like "a sea in a heavy gale," because of the many mountain ranges zigzagging across the peninsula. These divide the country into regions, often with different dialects and customs. The Taebaek mountain range runs down the eastern side of the country forming a rocky coastline. Jirisan is Korea's highest mainland peak at 6,283 feet (1,915 m), but even higher is the dormant volcano, Hallasan. Hallasan is on Jeju Island off the south coast, and rises to 6,398 feet (1,950 m).

▼ *Mount Sorek, the third-highest mountain in South Korea, is a popular destination for tourists, especially in the fall.*

PLACE IN THE WORLD

Total area: 38,023 sq miles (98,480 sq km)

Percentage of world land area: 0.07%

World ranking: 108th

▲ *Haenyeo divers on Jeju Island haul in their catch of shellfish. The seas around the island are overflowing with life.*

Islands

Korea sits on an ancient land bridge that is slowly tilting west toward the Yellow Sea. Throughout the years, this movement has helped to create over 3,000 islands off the western coastline. The largest island is Jeju Island, which was formed by volcanic eruptions. The west coast has one of the world's biggest tidal ranges—the difference between high and low tide can be as much as 30 feet (9 m).

IT'S A FACT!

For the last 20 years, Jeju Island has been a favorite honeymoon destination for South Koreans, thanks to its warm climate and spectacular volcanic scenery. The island is also famous for its *haenyeo*, or diving women, who plunge below the waves in search of shellfish and sea urchins.

Climate

South Korea has four distinct seasons. Winter is bitterly cold, thanks to icy winds that blow down from Siberia. Spring is a time of change; by June, monsoon winds blow from the south. They bring warm, wet weather, causing the Korean summer to be hot and humid. The rainy season, *changma*, lasts from late June to late July. Towards the end of the summer, typhoons arrive from the south, and strong winds are common throughout fall.

▲ *The rainy season can bring serious flooding to South Korea in the hot summer months.*

Natural Hazards

Powerful storms called typhoons lash the South Korean coastline every year. In 2003, Typhoon Maemi caused enormous damage to the city of Pusan. More than 25,000 people were left homeless and 117 died, including 28 passengers who were killed when a landslide knocked a train off its tracks. More than 460 ships were either sunk or marooned. Large areas of farmland were flooded, ruining South Korea's rice harvest.

THE HOME OF...

Ginseng

Korean ginseng originally grew wild in the forests, but is now grown on farms. It is thought to be the best in the world. Once valued more highly than gold, the herb is used as a cure in traditional medicine. In the past, ginseng roots were eaten raw. Now, South Koreans enjoy it in jelly, candy, energy drinks, and chewing gum.

Endangered Wildlife

Over 65 percent of South Korea is covered by forest. Despite this, not many large animals live in the wild. The Korean tiger is now extinct, and wildcats, lynxes, and small Korean bears survive in minimal numbers. A wild dog unique to Korea, the Jindo Gae, lives on the island of Jin. South Korea is also home to many beautiful water birds. The Manchurian crane, a national symbol, was thought to be extinct. However, in 1977 some of these birds were found living in the demilitarized zone.

▼ *South Korea's Buddhist temples are set in beautifully designed and tended landscapes. They are peaceful places, suitable for Buddhist contemplation.*

IT'S A FACT!

For centuries, Buddhist monks lovingly tended the gardens in temples, which were home to many of the finest specimens of trees and plants in South Korea. The gardens were designed to be as natural as possible with lotus ponds, terraced flower beds, and streams running throughout.

Population and Migration

There is not much flat land in South Korea, so 80 percent of its population live in large cities along the south and west coasts. Almost all South Koreans belong to the same ethnic group. Apart from the 20,000 Chinese inhabitants, there are no large minorities.

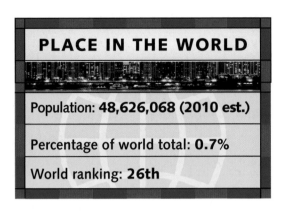

PLACE IN THE WORLD

Population: **48,626,068 (2010 est.)**

Percentage of world total: **0.7%**

World ranking: **26th**

Fast-growing Cities

Since the 1960s, South Korean cities have grown very quickly. Along the Han River in Seoul, there are thousands of high-rise buildings reaching 20 to 30 stories high. These were built to house migrants from the country to the city. Each building is similar to a small village with rooms for the elderly, kindergartens for children, and clubs for housewives. During the 1990s, some buildings were built too quickly. A department store collapsed in Seoul in 1995 killing 500 people—the biggest peacetime disaster in South Korean history.

▼ *Along the Han River in Seoul stand hundreds of high-rise buildings—the homes and offices of its 10.4 million inhabitants.*

▲ *This huge Korean supermarket caters to the large Korean community in Maryland.*

IT'S A FACT!

Over 40 cities in South Korea have more than 100,000 inhabitants. Around 30 percent of South Korea's population lives in just three cities: Seoul, Pusan, and Incheon. The streets are crowded, and South Korea has one of the worst air-pollution problems in the world. Green parks in the cities are few and far between. Worried that its capital Seoul was growing too big, the South Korean government has developed new satellite cities such as Gwacheon, Bucheon, and Bundang.

Overseas Population

Today, around 7 million Koreans live abroad. More than one-third live in the United States. They are known for being hard-working, running many grocery stores in big cities. During the late 19th century, many Koreans migrated to China, and almost 2 million of their descendants live there today. Around 600,000 Koreans live in Japan, mainly the result of 1.25 million Koreans being forced to work in Japanese mines and factories during World War II. In recent years, professional "matchmakers" have become increasingly common, matching up Koreans working overseas with possible husbands or wives back in South Korea.

In South Korea, ancient traditions sit alongside a dynamic modern culture. In the past, Korea was strongly influenced by the religion, language, and art of China. In turn, it passed these ideas on to Japan. Then Korea closed its doors to the outside world. In the last 200 years, however, it has absorbed many Western ideas.

◀ *Young Koreans wear modern fashions and use the latest technology, but they also respect the ancient traditions of their country.*

IT'S A FACT!

The South Korean flag shows a circle divided into two parts on a white background. One side is called the *yin*, which stands for the positive things in nature. The other side is called *yang*, the negative things. This symbol comes from the ancient Chinese philosopher Confucius and shows how things can be equal, but opposite.

A Mix of Old and New

At first sight, people in Seoul seem much like any other modern city-dwellers, wearing suits and modern fashions to work and using cell phones. But underneath, many old ways remain. By nature, Koreans are patient, flexible, and have a sense of fun. They follow a code of politeness known as *gibun*, and try to avoid arguments. For example, young Koreans on a crowded bus are quick to give up their seat for an elderly passenger.

The Korean Language

Koreans have their own language, spoken by 65 million people throughout the Korean Peninsula. Different dialects are spoken in different parts of the country, though the dialect of Jeju Island is so strong that some people regard it as a separate language. Koreans write using the Hangul alphabet. Unlike Chinese written symbols, the 24 Hangul letters express sounds rather than things and ideas. South Korea is the only country in the world with a national holiday celebrating its writing—Hangul Day.

▼ *This sign on a fast-food restaurant shows the unique shape of Korean letters.*

FAMOUS SOUTH KOREAN

King Sejong (1397–1450)

At first, Korean scholars used Chinese symbols to write. Then in 1443, King Sejong the Great introduced Hangul, the Korean alphabet. This made it much easier for everyone to read and write Korean, as no one had to spend years learning Chinese symbols. King Sejong's portrait still appears everywhere, even on the 10,000-won note!

Religion and Beliefs

Around 1,500 years ago, Buddhism became the official religion in Korea. It is still one of the two main religions in South Korea, along with Christianity. More than 45 percent of South Koreans say they have no religion at all. However, many still follow the ideas of the Chinese philosopher, Confucius. The Korean calendar is based on lunar months, and South Koreans enjoy at least one major celebration during each moon. Traditional clothing and food are a part of Korean celebrations, which honor ancestors, elders, and religious figures.

A Mobile Life

Life for modern South Koreans is based around their cell phones. It is common to see South Koreans of all ages sitting in trains and buses watching TV or reading comic books on their phones. South Koreans increasingly use "T-money"—electronic cash stored on SIM cards and other phone cards—instead of credit cards or cash.

IT'S A FACT!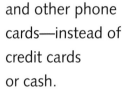

Family is very important in South Korean culture. Many South Korean families create memorial shrines for their dead relatives, which they visit on special days. During the Lunar and Harvest Moon festivals, up to 20 million South Korean people may visit these graves in their home towns. The royal shrines in the Jeongjeon in Seoul are the oldest Confucian shrines in the world and a popular tourist attraction.

▶ *Buddha's birthday is celebrated with a street festival and a parade of lanterns in the shape of lotus flowers, dragons, elephants, and buddhas. Buddhists come from all over Asia to celebrate in Seoul.*

▲ *Children offer their teacher flowers as part of Teacher's Day, celebrated on May 15.*

Growing Up in South Korea

South Korean children are named in a special ceremony 100 days after they are born. They are given pencils and thread, which are the symbols for wisdom and long life. Education in South Korea is free, and children and teenagers study hard to be successful in school and beyond. In their free time, they enjoy chatting with friends, watching TV, or listening to the latest pop music. Children's Day, celebrated on May 5, is like Christmas for South Korean children. It is a time of presents and fun. The Korean children's writer,

GLOBAL LEADER

Education

South Korea has one of the best education systems in the world. All children must attend to the age of 11, and 97 percent graduate from high school—more than any other country in the world. Mathematics, science, Korean, and English are the most important subjects. South Korea also has the world's highest estimated national IQ—a way of rating a person's intelligence.

Bang Jeong-hwan, created this national holiday in 1923 to give children a sense of pride in themselves and their country.

Traditional Arts

Arts are an important part of South Korea's past and present. Music, dancing, and theater were all performed in palaces, while country people enjoyed folk dances in colorful costumes. Traditional dancing is still performed at official ceremonies, and in the last 50 years, folk arts have become popular again. Traditional Korean drummers are famous worldwide. South Koreans love to dance and sing, and many streets have a song room for karaoke. The art of calligraphy—handwriting using brushes—is a popular hobby.

◀ *Traditional dancing and costumes are an important part of ceremonies and festivals.*

Sports

South Koreans enjoy many sports, including badminton, golf, soccer, and skiing. Fishing and hiking in the mountains are also very popular. Others enjoy traditional sports such as *yutnori*, a game of tossing sticks that is more than 2,000 years old. Kite-flying contests were originally invented for soldiers to practice battle tactics. In these contests, competitors try to cut each other's silk strings.

GOING GLOBAL

South Korean TV programs, films, and music are very popular across Asia, especially in China. In fact, the "Korean Wave," as it is known, is now reaching across the world. South Korean TV dramas and movies are watched in countries from Iran and the Philippines to Mexico and Argentina. Big singing stars include TVXQ, Rain, and BoA.

IT STARTED HERE

Tae Kwon Do

The martial art of tae kwon do started in Korea more than 1,000 years ago. Tae kwon do means "the way of the fist and foot." It combines fighting skills with exercise, meditation, and philosophy, and it is used by the South Korean army as part of its training. It has been an Olympic sport since 2000.

▶ *While Olympic tae kwon do is about speed and attack, the traditional art is more about power and self-defense.*

Food and Drink

No Korean celebration is complete without traditional foods. Rice is eaten with all meals in South Korea. Many dishes have vegetables in them, such as *kimchi*, which is pickled cabbage mixed with peppers and garlic. Fish, shellfish, and seaweed are also prepared in many different ways. People eat using chopsticks, but spoons are also used for rice and soup. Adults enjoy several popular alcoholic drinks, including *makgeolli*, a milky drink made from rice, and *soju*, made from potatoes. However, food tastes are changing in South Korea, and many young people also enjoy burgers and pizza.

Economy and Trade

South Korea was once a poor country that relied on farming and fishing. By the 1990s, it had become one of the world's leading industrial countries and was one of the four "Asian Tigers," along with Singapore, Taiwan, and Hong Kong. South Korea remains a world leader in high-tech electronic goods, information technology, steel, car-making, and shipbuilding.

GLOBAL LEADER

Shipbuilding

South Korea is a major center for heavy industry. The Pohang Iron and Steel Company is the world's second-largest steel producer. In 2008, firms in South Korea built more ships than the rest of the world put together. The world's largest shipyard in Ulsan (owned by Hyundai) is so efficient that it can build a huge ship in only four days.

Growth of an Asian Tiger

The economic success of South Korea is known as the "Miracle on the Han." It is based on the good education system in the country and a highly skilled workforce.

▼ *The Ulsan shipyard is the largest in the world, employing more than 35,000 people.*

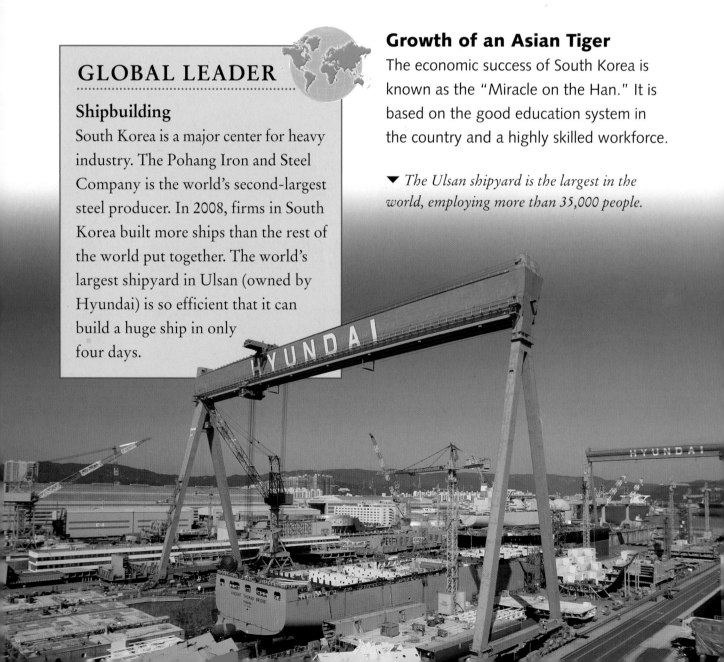

The country also became rich by exporting to countries such as Australia, the United Kingdom, and the United States. In 2008, South Korea was the world's eleventh-biggest exporter. The government has encouraged large, family-owned firms, known as *jaebol*. The biggest of these are known all over the world. Samsung makes electronic goods, while Hyundai-Kia makes ships and cars.

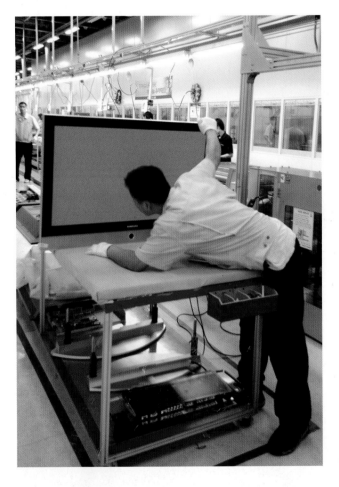

▲ *South Korean firm Samsung is one of the world's leading electronics manufacturers. Here, a man works on an assembly line making plasma-screen TVs.*

IT STARTED HERE

Battleships

Cut off from most of Asia by land, South Korea has always been a seafaring nation. The first battleships covered in iron were built in Korea in the 1590s. They were known as "turtles" due to their thick "shells." The metal plates held jagged spikes and knives to prevent enemies from boarding. The turtles helped the Korean Admiral Yi Sun-sin defeat a Japanese invasion of Korea between 1592 and 1598.

The Economy Today

The South Korean economy is now the third-largest in Asia. Since 2008, however, it has been badly hit by the world banking crisis. As a big exporter, South Korea is also affected by the economic problems in China, Japan, and the United States. South Koreans are paid more than workers in emerging economies such as China and Vietnam. In the past, high wages have put some South Korean firms out of business. Some experts worry that as Korea's population is growing older, it will be harder for the economy to keep growing, as more people will be retiring without enough young people to take over their jobs.

Car Industry

Fifty years ago, the car industry in South Korea assembled parts made in Japan and the United States. During the 1990s, it proved it could build its own quality cars. Today, Hyundai-Kia is the world's sixth-largest car manufacturer. Although car sales have fallen due to the global economic crisis, the South Korean government is investing huge amounts of money into developing cars for the future. These include hybrid cars with both electric and gas engines, and intelligent cars that slow down when they get close to the car in front.

GLOBAL LEADER

Working Hours

South Korea is perhaps the hardest-working nation in the world. The average employee works 2,357 hours per year. That's six-and-a-half hours for every single day of their lives (including holidays). Children go to school 6 days a week, 220 days a year. Children in the United States go to school 5 days a week, 180 days a year.

▼ *Men work on a car assembly in the Hyundai factory.*
The car industry is one of the most important in South Korea.

▲ Tourists gather to watch the changing of the guards ceremony at the royal palace in Seoul.

PLACE IN THE WORLD

Value of economy:
US$929,121 million

Percentage of world total: **1.5%**

World ranking: **15th**

Tourism

More than 6 million foreign tourists visit South Korea each year, most of them from Japan, China, and Hong Kong. This is partly due to Asian interest in Korean culture. South Korea is connected by 1,864 miles (3,000 km) of railways and 1,243 miles (2,000 km) of highways, so most of the country lies within a day's round trip of the big cities. Popular attractions include the capital Seoul, the ancient capitals of Kyongju and Buyeo, the beautiful mountain scenery, and islands such as Jeju.

High-tech Center

Thanks to its high-tech IT network, South Korea has been called "the most wired country on the planet." It has led the way in high-speed and wireless Internet services. By 2009, almost every household had a high-speed Internet connection. In 2005, South Korea became the first country in the world where cell phones could receive digital television signals. This new technology brings its own problems, however. In 2009, hackers used viruses to attack web sites belonging to a government security agency and major banks in South Korea.

Government and Politics

In the past, Korea has been conquered by Mongols, Russians, and Japanese. After World War II, the Korean Peninsula was split in two: democratic South Korea and communist North Korea. Today, South Korea is a republic, which means it is not ruled by a king or queen but by an elected government. The president is head of state, while the prime minister leads the government in parliament.

Japanese Rule

In 1910, Japan conquered Korea. Japanese rule was tough on the Koreans. They had to speak Japanese in public and adopt Japanese names and beliefs. Although the Japanese helped to modernize the country by building highways, railways, and ports, they also took over large areas of farmland and owned all the factories. At the end of World War II, the American army recaptured the south and the Russian army recaptured the north. In 1948, a boundary line was drawn between the two halves.

▼ *South Koreans celebrate the 90th anniversary of the Independence Movement, commemorating the beginning of the resistance against Japanese occupation.*

FAMOUS SOUTH KOREAN

Yu Kwan-Sun
(1902–20)

Yu Kwan-Sun was a 16-year-old student in 1919 when she organized a mass demonstration against the Japanese occupation of Korea. Both her parents were shot by the Japanese police during the demonstration and Yu was arrested. Although she was tortured in prison, Yu continued her protests until she died in 1920.

▲ *Korean and American soldiers in an observation tower in the DMZ—the dividing line between North and South Korea.*

North vs South

In 1950, war broke out between South Korea, supported by the United States and other democracies, and North Korea, supported by the communist Soviet Union and China. No treaty was signed at the end of the war in 1953, so the Korean Peninsula remains divided. The war had a terrible effect. Many cities were reduced to rubble and around 300,000 South Koreans died. Two million died in North Korea. Since the war, South Korea has become wealthy, but North Korea remains one of the poorest countries in the world.

IT'S A FACT!

In 1953, at the end of the Korean War, the boundary between South and North Korea was established. Known as the demilitarized zone, or DMZ, this strip of land cuts the Korean Peninsula in half. It runs 154 miles (248 km) from east to the west, and remains the most heavily fortified border in the world. In keeping so many soldiers on guard, the South Korean armed forces has grown to the sixth-largest in the world.

The Army Takes Over

In the 1960s, the South Korean army took control of the country. From 1961 until 1979, South Korea was led by General Park Chung Hee. Though Park's rule was harsh, the economy grew rapidly. He encouraged the development of the giant family-run companies called *jaebol*. Park was assassinated in 1979, but democracy wasn't restored until 1987. In 1992, Kim Young-Sam became South Korea's first civilian president.

Sunshine Policy

In 2000, the leaders of North and South Korea met and tried to make up their differences. This attempt at peaceful cooperation was known as the Sunshine policy. One hundred North Koreans met their relatives in the South in a very emotional reunion. In May 2007, trains connected the two nations for the first time in 56 years. In 2010, however, ties were cut after North Korea was accused of sinking a South Korean ship and attacking a civilian area.

▲ *South Korean companies employ thousands of North Korean workers at the Kaesong industrial complex near the border.*

GOING GLOBAL

North Korea's recent nuclear missile and underground bomb tests are very worrying for South Korea. Luckily, it has strong military support from the United States, its main ally since 1954. There are currently 30,000 U.S. troops based in South Korea. However, not all South Koreans are happy with the size of the U.S. forces in their country. In 2006, there were violent protests outside the U.S. base at Camp Humphreys.

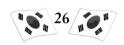

International Links

As a big exporter, South Korea works hard to stay on good terms with the rest of the world. Since the Korean War in the 1950s, it has had strong links with the U.S. In 2007, South Korea signed a Free Trade Agreement with the U.S. to encourage trade with one of its largest markets. In August 1991, South Korea joined the United Nations; the same time North Korea joined. It is also a member of the G20 group of economically powerful nations, which it led in 2010.

▼ *Diplomat Ban Ki-Moon in his office at the United Nations.*

FAMOUS SOUTH KOREAN

Ban Ki-Moon (b. 1944)

South Korean Ban Ki-Moon is the head of the UN. As a boy, Ban would walk 6 miles (9.7 km) to a local factory to practice English with its American staff. At 18, he won an essay competition, which earned him a trip to the United States. As Secretary-General of the UN, Ban has reformed its peacekeeping operations. He has also repeatedly and urged the world's nations to combat global warming.

South Korea in 2020

South Korea has transformed itself over the past 50 years, and there is every reason to believe it will remain a strong economic force in Asia. It was one of the quickest to recover after the Asian economic crisis in 1997 when the Korean government invested heavily in the high-tech industry to solve the country's problems.

High-tech Center

Many experts agree that the future of computers lies in South Korea and other Asian countries. U.S. firms turn to South Korea to try out their latest products. There is nowhere in Korea without a cell phone signal. Many South Koreans carry a gadget called a "ubiquitous robotic companion," or URC, which allows them to connect to the Internet wherever they are.

▼ *Technology will continue to improve South Korea's economy. This is a demonstration of the latest in robot technology at a fair in Seoul.*

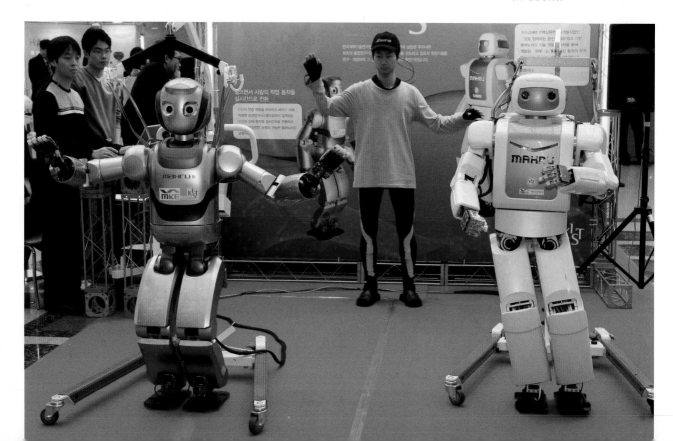

▲ *A large solar farm is opened on the South Korean island of Jeju in 2009. The country is taking large steps towards more environmentally friendly energy sources.*

A Greener Future

South Korea is the twelfth-largest emitter of carbon dioxide in the world. This greenhouse gas, created by burning fossil fuels such as oil and coal, is a major contributor to global warming. Meanwhile, more and more energy is being used in South Korea. However, the South Korean government is investing lots of money in eco-friendly projects. These include plans to clean up the country's four major rivers, make homes more energy-efficient, and build transportation networks that use less energy.

GLOBAL LEADER

Renewable Energy

A state-of-the-art renewable energy village has been built on the island of Jeju. On the roof of each of the 40 houses in Donggwang village are beds of solar panels. Even the small local elementary school runs on free electric energy from the sun. The solar panels produce enough energy to power the entire area.

Hopes of Peace?

A historic meeting between the leaders of North and South Korea in 2007 led to hopes that the two countries might one day agree on a permanent truce. But the continuing threat from North Korea—especially its nuclear missile tests—makes this unlikely in the near future. Also, the United States, which maintains tens of thousands of soldiers in South Korea, may pull its forces away from the DMZ by 2020.

Glossary

Asian Tigers the name given to rapidly growing economies in Asia, including South Korea, Hong Kong, Singapore, and Taiwan.

Buddhism a religion that follows the teachings of Buddha (c. 563–483 BC), and involves studying wisdom, meditation, and following an ethical code.

civilian someone who is not a member of the military.

Communism the political and social system in countries with a ruling Communist Party where all property is owned by the state; food and supplies are given out to the people.

democracy a type of government where people vote for the people they wish to represent them.

dialect the way a language is spoken by a group of people, such as the words they use and the way they pronounce them.

economy the financial system of a country or region, including how much money is made from the production and sale of goods and services.

ethnic group a group of people who identify with each other and feel they share a history.

export to send or transport products or materials abroad for sale or trade.

fossil fuels fuels made from the remains of plants and animals that died millions of years ago; coal, oil, and natural gas are all fossil fuels.

global warming the gradual rise in temperatures on the surface of the Earth.

greenhouse gas a gas that traps heat in the atmosphere, which can contribute to global warming.

hacker a computer expert who uses their skill to break into computer systems illegally.

IQ a measure of how intelligent a person is; the higher someone's IQ, the more intelligent they are considered to be.

karaoke a form of entertainment in which popular songs are sung to recorded music.

migrants people who move from one place to another to live or work.

nuclear weapons bombs and other explosive weapons that get their power from nuclear reactions.

peninsula a large area of land that juts out into a body of water such as a sea or ocean.

pollution harmful materials that damage the air, water, and soil, such as vehicle emissions, waste gases from factories, or chemicals from fertilizers.

satellite cities cities close to major cities that are designed to take the overspill of the population.

United Nations (UN) an organization of the world's countries that promotes peace across the globe.

Further Information

Books

South Korea
Countries of the World
by Tom Jackson
(National Geographic, 2007)

Korea
Now and Then: A View Through Time
by Marylou Morano Kjelle
(Mitchell Lane Publishers, 2010)

South Korea
Country Explorers
by Jennifer A. Miller
(Lerner, 2010)

South Korea
Enchantment of the World. Second series.
by Patricia K. Kummer
(Children's Press, 2008)

Web Sites

http://kids.nationalgeographic.com/Places/Find/South-korea
National Geographic's page on South Korea for kids, packed with facts and photos.

http://www.timeforkids.com/TFK/kids/hh/goplaces/main/0,28375,927166,00.html
The Time for Kids guide to South Korea, where you can take a virtual journey around the country and even learn the language,

https://www.cia.gov/library/publications/the-world-factbook/geos/ks.html
This World Factbook entry provides information on the history, people, government, economy, geography, communications, transportation, and military of South Korea.

Every effort has been made by the publisher to ensure that these web sites contain no inappropriate or offensive material. However, because of the nature of the Internet, it is impossible to guarantee that the content of these sites will not be altered. We strongly advise that Internet access is supervised by a responsible adult.

Index

Numbers in **bold** indicate pictures